DEPRESSION
and its
REMEDY

Wim Malgo

Translated by
Roger J. Elmore

Midnight Call, Incorporated
Columbia, South Carolina
U.S.A.

Manufactured in the United States of America
ISBN 0-937422-03-7

Introduction

The Twentieth Century Industrial Revolution has created numerous psychological and mental effects on humanity which no one can deny. Human nature is too often "incapable" to usurp the complex of requests and pressures asserted on him in this twentieth century. One of the most obvious symptoms in modern society is the undefinable fear of things which are to come. This fear has captured millions of people around the world and lead them into an ever-deepening bondage of depression. With this book, the author attempts to show the cause and the remedy for depression in a simple Bible-based way. Depression and its related symptoms can, and have been, successfully repaired by dedicated psychiatrists, psychologists, and other professionals. However, the author's intention is not attempting to pass on helpful hints on how to cope or relieve depression, but rather shows a simple way as to how one can be completely redeemed from depression. The Bible's claim, "behold, I make all things new" can and must become a reality in the life of one who is suffering under depression. Thus, this book is not based upon scientific research or study, but rather on the simplicity of the unfailing Word of God, which in itself, has the power to liberate and to renew — NOT on a temporary basis, but for eternity!

Contents

Depression and its Remedy

Wim Malgo

Chapter I

Where to Go to Cure Your Depression?

Expressed concretely: to Jesus! What does that mean? It means accept His invitation which is valid today: *"Come unto me, all ye that labour and are heavy laden, and I will give you rest."* Are you asking yourself: Does this apply to me, too? Yes, because He repeatedly said: *"Him that cometh to me I will in no wise cast out."* Jesus not only invites you to come to Him, but He also comes to you. At least make the effort to read John's gospel through once! In this reference we find a concrete example in chapter 5:

Hope for the Hopeless

In the five halls by the pool of Bethesda in Jerusalem there was a lame man who had

lain there among the many sick persons for
38 years. There was something special about
the pool of Bethesda: As John reports, an
angel periodically descended and stirred the
water. Whoever of the sick persons was the
first to climb into the water when this
happened was cured. One time when Jesus
was walking through these halls. He saw the
lame man who, in his despair, had already
been lying there for 38 years, and He asked
him: *"Wilt thou be made whole?"* The man
answered in an astonished way which
reflected his resignation: *"Sir, I have no man,
when the water is troubled, to put me into the
pool: but while I am coming, another steppeth
down before me."* Jesus responds with a wonderful answer which freed him from his
despair: *"Rise, take up thy bed, and walk. And
immediately the man was made whole, and he
took up his bed and walked, and on the same
day was the sabbath."*

Bethesda lay nine meters (about 30 feet)
below the earth's surface because those who
conquered Jerusalem again and again built
on top of the ruins. But now one can see the
ruins of the five halls of Bethesda, and even

Bethesda today: Several of the halls are visible. The pool was at the very bottom.

the pool, because this area has been completely excavated.

The Greatest Physician
and Inner Sickness

Why did Jesus ask this lame man if he wanted to be made whole? There must be a deeper reason for this, because He, the Son of God, never says a word too much or a word too less. This deeper reason was that this man's spirit was dazed, and any hope he had had for healing and deliverance was extinguished. Despair had so completely taken control of his personality that he could no longer hope. Every time the angel descended into the water and stirred it, he had hoped he would, at some time, be the first one into the water, and be healed. But he never managed to do it. He waited and hoped until he completely lost heart, and dejection had robbed his spirit of its strength. Things like this can happen in the life of a person until he reaches the point where he is in complete despair.

Jesus touched upon the heart of this man's decades-long need when He asked His question. He plucked a string within him whose sound had long since died away. The

Excavated ruins of the temple where Jesus did not even receive a word of thanks from the man He healed at Bethesda.

Lord can do the same thing right now in your hopeless, despairing heart! Jesus is greater and more powerful than the angel which periodically descended into this pool.

Bethesda means "House of Mercy." Jesus is merciful. But this fact alone does not answer the question why He happened to meet just this man and ask him: *"Wilt thou be made whole?"* It is often maintained that the Lord healed all the physically-ill people He encountered, but this is not true. Otherwise the five halls of Bethesda would immediately have become empty. There is a large variety of blessed reasons why God often permits His children to remain sick. But why did Jesus ask the question of this man: *"Wilt thou be made whole?"* Answer: His body had been lame for so long because years earlier this spirit had been stained and lamed by sin! You ask how I know that? I assume this to be true because of the statement Jesus later made in the temple to the man who had been healed: *"Behold, thou art made whole: sin no more, lest a worse thing come unto thee."* Surely you will agree with me when I say that this man did not fully understand the implications of Jesus' question: *"Wilt thou be made whole?,"* because his first reaction after he had been healed proves this. In John 5 it says: *"Jesus saith unto him, Rise, take up thy bed, and walk. And immediately the man was made whole, and took up his bed, and walked."* Although a great deal happened to this man outwardly, nothing happened inwardly! He lacked thanks and surrender. We wait in vain for the question: "Lord, who are you?" It is exactly the same today with millions of people. Outwardly they have experienced great miracles, but inwardly they are still sick. Later, in the temple, when Jesus informed the man who had been healed of the reason for his sickness — sin — instead of falling down before the Lord and asking Him to forgive him for his sins, he went to the religious authorities and betrayed Him! The Bible says: *"The man departed, and told the Jews that it was Jesus, which had made him whole. And therefore did the Jews persecute Jesus, and sought to slay him, because he had done these things on the sabbath day."*

The Lord Jesus healed many other sick people as He wandered upon the earth. Once He even healed a man sick of palsy. As a consequence of this person's inward frame of mind, Jesus could help him, first of all, inwardly — in contrast to the lame man of Bethesda — and then outwardly, too. We read this in the gospel of Matthew: *"And, behold, they brought to him a man sick of the palsy, lying on a bed: and Jesus seeing their faith said unto the sick of the palsy; Son, be of good*

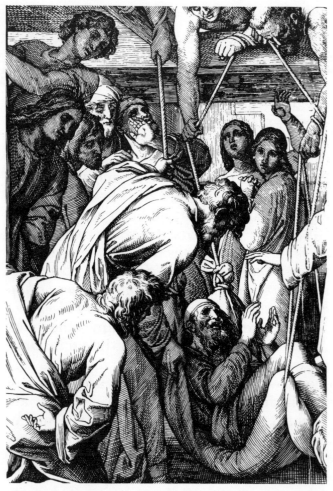

Forgiving the sins of the man sick of palsy (Matthew 9:2), who was later healed by Jesus.

cheer, thy sins be forgiven thee." Later the Lord also healed him of his physical illness by commanding him: *"Arise, take up thy bed, and go unto thine house."* So many people today are glad to let themselves be helped outwardly, but not inwardly.

Now that we have seen that Jesus' question to the lame man was not only significant, but was necessary, I would like to ask you the same question at His command:

Whilt Thou Be Made Whole?

Jesus does not ask: "Wilt thou be saved from the eternal torment of hell?" You would certainly say "yes" to this question, because everyone would like to go to heaven. If one were to ask a man who had been sentenced to death: "Would you like to escape being executed?," we know what his answer would be. He would say: "Oh, yes, I beg for mercy!" But the question which Jesus asks you very personally goes deeper: *"Wilt thou be made whole?"* This means: "Do you repent with all your heart? Will you become a new person?" Only Jesus can help you! But He first wants to heal you inwardly.

Completely Whole

There have been only three people on earth who were completely whole in body, soul and spirit: Adam and Eve — before the fall from grace — and Jesus Christ. The first two were perfect, without sin, until Satan misled them into sin. But Jesus never sinned. He never injured anyone, either with words or deeds. Because He said a resounding "no" to every type of sin, He was not contaminated by it, even when in the midst of the most sinful persons! Jesus was neither a passing-through-station for sin, but a terminal station. No one could assert that He had committed even a single sin.

Oh, how quickly we are polluted by the surrounding world! But Jesus, God's Son, was separated from sin. Nevertheless, did He boast of this? Did He say to the Pharisees: "Depart from me, because I am holier than thou?" No, on the contrary. It is exactly because He was separated from sin, and took no part in shady dealings, that He ate and drank with sinners, touched them in blessing with His hands, and healed many sick persons.

Jesus, the Son of God, became man, just like you and I. He became like us in all things. He was tempted like us, but in contrast to us, He never sinned. Would you like to become like Jesus?

That is God's Goal for You

It is God's wish, not only that we receive eternal life through faith in Jesus Christ, but His chief goal is becoming like Him. He wants us to become like His Son, Jesus, that we turn our backs on sin in all its forms. Why? Because God created man in His own image. Adam was perfect, like God. But he let himself be led into sin, and sin caused God's image in him to be obscured, and then completely lost. You are Adam's offspring, and for that reason the hereditary image of sin is part of your nature.

But Jesus could say: *"He that hath seen me hath seen the Father."* Anyone who accepts Jesus in faith, who provides a dwelling place for Him in his heart, is transformed back into the image of God, because he is transformed into the image of Jesus. That is God's plan and goal for you! But Satan wants to prevent this. Anyone who wants to reach God's goal for his

The hill of Golgotha (Place of the Skull), today in Jerusalem.

life, i.e., to become like His Son, will be ridiculed and derided like Jesus. But through this you will become one with Him, and despair departs from anyone who has become one with Jesus.

Think It Over

I know that among my readers there are those whose hearts are dominated by hopelessness and despair, and you do not know the remedy for it. Look, the Lord is standing before you: *"Wilt thou be made whole?"* He would like to make an exchange with you. If you say "yes" to Jesus, then the reversed pride within you, your self-admiration, will be eliminated, and that which is good, which you value so lightly, will be planted in you. Then He will give His life to you, and you may surrender your sinful life to Him. That is the exchange with Jesus. How did such an exchange ever become possible? Because Jesus bore the sins of the world on the cross of Calvary. Because God loved us so much that He "made him to be sin, who knew no sin" (His only begotten Son). I can well imagine that you are saying: "Yes, I want to be made whole and have eternal life. I want to be rid of my depression. Yes, I want very much to be like Jesus." But I must tell you: Think it over! If you really knew what Jesus is like and who He is, then I doubt whether you would strive for this goal with your whole will. In the case of many people who were converted I observed during my 33 years of ministering, that they did not realize until later how high a price must be paid to become like Jesus. You can achieve God's high goal for your life only if you completely surrender your life to Him! It is exactly here that powerful forces of resistance enter in, because many resist becoming one with Jesus on the cross. The apostle Paul was one who faithfully followed Jesus, and could say: *"I am crucified with Christ."* But still I ask you: "Wilt thou be made completely whole?"

Be True!

You can be made completely whole through love for absolute truth. Somewhere I once read the sentence "Only God is objective." That is a true statement. Only He is truth. The more we become one with Jesus, the more true we become. But in the case of many people today, they deviate from that which is really truth. In their eyes, mistakes made by others are crimes. Because of their untrue, sick nature, they quickly assume a bad opinion of others. "Wilt thou be healed of this sickness?" Are you willing, from this hour on, to speak only the truth about God and your fellow man? The Lord Jesus could rightly say of Himself: *"I am the truth."*

Many people would have very little to say if they were permitted to speak only the truth. How many untruths have you already uttered? *"Wilt thou be made whole?"* If you cannot forgive an insult, it is because your soul is sick. When someone tells you the truth, you strike back. But when you have been made whole, you are able to forgive anyone who offends or insults you. All desire for revenge on your enemies disappears, and you are filled with God's love. In Christ you become a new person. He says: *"Behold, I make all things new."*

There are terminally-ill Christians who love money more than they love Jesus Christ. If you were completely whole, you would have open hands, you would be charitable. But you are like the man of Bethesda who had been sick for 38 years, and had now been healed, but who did not have a word or act of thanks for Jesus. Do you want to be healed of your anger, your impurity, of your impatience? Do not boast about yourself! Do not brag about your so-called thriftiness which is nothing more than greed! Do not boast of your professional capability which only promotes pride! The Bible says: *"Who knowing the judgment of God; that they which commit such things are worthy of death, not only do the same, but have pleasure in them that do them."* Are you in this category? Do you boast about your sinful deeds, and do you feel glad about the vices of others? When Jesus calls to you now: *"Wilt thou be made whole?"* it is not only because of your condition, but also because He is returning soon! You do not have much more time! You do not know whether you will be alive tomorrow or not. Jesus wants to make everything about you new. But you have to say "yes" to Him! This great change in your life can happen today! Perhaps you must complain, just like that sick man: *"Sir, I have no man."* You, too, have been disappointed by those around you. People have left you in the lurch. They are all looking out for themselves, but Jesus will never leave you in the lurch. He says to everyone who has accepted Him in faith: *"Lo, I am with you alway."* I proclaim these words from the Bible to you: *"Seek ye the Lord while he may be found, call ye upon him while he is near."*

Chapter II

The Remedy
for Your Fear

Today millions upon millions of people are victims of fear. There are conditions of fear which one can transmit to others by means of unjust words and deeds. Illnesses, shortness of breath and other threatening dangers can also cause fear. Serious neuroses of fear are also produced by the world political situation, and even by fear of what the future holds for us.

Shortly before his death, the well-known journalist, W.S. Schlamm, wrote a book entitled: *The Spirit of Our Age is Suffering from Fear.* In this book he asserts: "The political and human wills of people in this time are not formed by knowledge, but by fear — fear, sheer fear, physical fear, determines personal relationships of both private and social natures. Fear of cancer, fear of the atom, fear of social conflict. Fear of bacteria, fear of kidnapping. Fear of pills and medicines. Fear of being regarded as peculiar. Fear of old age. Fear of taxes. Fear of fighting, fear of rain, snow, drought and heat, of automobile exhaust in the air and mercury in the fruit, of ocean pollution, of 'population explosion' and decrease in population. Fear of car breakdowns, a coming 'police state,' 'insects' and new elections, fear — naked, incessant fear.

This fear is being methodically and consistently promoted by all the 'media.' One cannot open a newspaper or turn on a TV set without being exposed to a stimulation of fear. This tortured spirit of the age is being produced by horror films, medical 'warnings' in the popular press, all the crime books, thrillers, comics, predictions of the future by Cassandra-like prophets of doom, 'citizen initiatives' against nuclear power plants, daily warnings about food and drink, about too much or too little exercise, gruesome reports about leukemia and heart attacks, life and death, about economic growth and economic crises, about anarchy on the one hand, and a 'police state' on the other, about poverty and wealth, 'emotions' and 'lack of contact.' 'Being informed,' 'being reasonable,' 'being rational' means to be afraid. 'Be afraid!' — that is basically all that 'public opinion' has to say to the individual. 'Be afraid!' — this is the first and only commandment of the spirit of this age.

Fear of life: Dead heroin addict in Rome. "The wages of sin is death."

A moment ago I said that this fear is being methodically and consistently promoted by all the 'media.' I did not mean by this that somewhere there is a group of macabre conspirators who plan all the fear strategies and who, thanks to the obedience of subordinate conspirators, have these strategies placed in the 'media.' Such hypotheses regarding all-knowing and all-powerful 'secret conspiracies.'

'The Wise Ones of Zion,' 'The Illuminati,' 'Wall Street,' 'multi-national companies,' 'world imperialism,' 'international banking capital' and all the other marketable nightmares are nothing more than an especially hysterical form of fear which causes us to lose our powers of reason. There are no 'secret conspiracies,' because in the entire history of the human race, only overt conspiracies have been successful — only conspiracies which with heroic (one could also say shameless) openness have confessed their goals — from the Gracchis to Lenin and Hitler. And there is no 'secret conspiracy' behind the 'fear strategy of our age. (No, behind it is inherent sin and the lack of desire to accept Jesus who

Fear of storms.

bore our sins on the cross of Calvary. One might also call this lack of desire a rejection of the fear of God. This is why man's fear is increasing. Author)." Schlamm further says, "From time immemorial religion has corresponded to this nature of man: It taught man to fear, hate and resist sin *within himself.* As long as man agreed, before God, to fear himself, he needed no other fear-causing stimuli (such as bacteria, viruses, nicotine, heart attacks, atoms, auto exhaust, 'insects,' weather, calories, cholesterol, aspirin, monarchies, policemen, bankers, terrorists, judges, politicians, etc.). Anyone who fears God on the one hand, and original sin on the other, fears nothing else in the world.

But it is well-known that 'God is dead,' and for this reason a great fear in a multitude of forms has broken out upon mankind. Soren Kierkegaard (1813-1855) knew all this, but he was only partially able to pass this knowledge on to a few philosophers who were, for the most part, 'existentialists.'

But Karl Marx, who was born in 1818, brilliantly understood how to give direction to this existential fear which was erupting everywhere (supposedly, author) and to use it as a political and social tool. In this century Marxism has fascinated the intelligence, and the intelligentsia is that social group which dominates the 'media,' the schools, all churches and social organisms which form

... of accidents.

the human consciousness. This 'intelligence' comprehends spontaneously, without any kind of secret direction, that motivations and object-goals must be given to this ever-present fear, because otherwise . . . because otherwise man, who *must* fear something, would reach God, or even worse, gain the understanding that communism is the arch-enemy, because modern man's only mean-ingful fear (apart from fear of God) would be the completely realistic fear of communist expansion. This is the only realistic fear, because man could actually do something against the spread of communism, while all the other fears produced by the spirit of our age are concerned with conditions which basically cannot be affected by the human will. Thank God that bacteria, viruses, atoms, the weather, life and death are independent of the human will. These phenomena do not care if they please us or not. Man has formative power only over himself and his relationships to other people, i.e., only over societal relations, and not over

. . . of collisions.

conditions and structures beyond his power. Fear about earthly dangers is rational only when man can efficiently act against it, as for example, fear of communism, and the activities of communism directed against him.

But the spirit of this age, or at least the 'intelligence' which represents it, desires that this one rational fear not emerge. Any other fear would be fine! As long as man's need to fear something can be satisfied with atoms, viruses, bacteria, aging, illness, weather and death, they will not have the dangerous fear of communism, and they will not work against it. That is more or less the conscious reason the public is supplied with the usual fear-producing stimuli. No one is 'secretly' formulating this strategy for fear — this is dependably done by the decadent instinct of an 'intelligence' which, out of pure sympathy for the revolution, plays up to man. Filled with fear as he is, man is ready to be swallowed up." This is what W.S. Schlamm says.

In spite of his clear explanation, we are only partly in agreement with him, because

Fear of war. Military cemetery in Holland.

the deep roots of fear do not come from communism, which is also a scourge of humanity, but from an unavoidable and inescapable encounter with the living God.

It is true that fear is greatly intensified by the mass media, but most people suffer from an indefinable fear, a fear which completely absorbs and consumes you, a fear which drives you. Fear in the morning, in the evening and during the night. Where does it come from? The definition of this fear is;

Sins Which Have Not Been Forgiven

Among these, for example, is the sin of idolatry, which means that you love and worship something or someone more than the Lord, who alone is worthy of worship. You worship your money, your house, your car, your children, your wife or husband, etc. It is your deep indebtedness, your unforgiven sins, which cause your inexpressible fears.

Israel was threatened with this awful fear when it would not obey God: *"And ye shall flee when none pursueth you."* And: *"And the sound of a shaken leaf shall chase them; and they shall flee, as fleeing from a sword; and they shall fall when none pursueth."* That is the fear which can only be characterized as "unpunished sin."

Do Not Be Afraid!

The one and only commandment of the spirit of this age is: "Be afraid!" But there is One who has overcome the world, and in so doing, has also overcome all fear: Jesus. Come with your fear to Him who repeatedly said: *"Fear not!"* Come with all your fears to Jesus who said: *"Let not your heart be troubled: ye believe in God, believe also in me."* But Jesus also said: *"I am the light of the world: he that followeth me shall not walk in darkness, but shall have the light of life."* By these lines He invites you to come to the light.

So come to the light, to Jesus — and confess your sins to Him, and His blood will cleanse you from all sin so that you can rejoice with the psalmist: *"Thou art my hiding place; thou shalt preserve me from trouble; thou shalt compass me about with songs of deliverance."*

Chapter III

Salvation Through Atomic Fission

Today there are false prophets in many countries. By means of their deceptive prophecies they are misleading countless people and bringing them to a state of despair; many have already taken their lives. Most of these prophecies have proven false because they are not of divine origin.

But everything predicted by the prophets of the Bible was and is literally being fulfilled. Over 1900 years ago, a simple fisherman named Peter prophesied: *"The Lord is not slack concerning his promise, as some men count slackness; but is long suffering to us-ward, not willing that any should perish, but that all should come to repentance."* And then he made the prediction which, at that time, was unbelievable: *"But the day of the Lord will come as a thief in the night; in which the heavens shall pass away with a great noise, and the* **elements shall melt** *with fervent heat, the earth also and the works that are therein shall be burned up."* Peter knew nothing of technology or physics. He had no idea of the possibility that man one day would split matter and that the elements would be melted in the process. Peter was no scientist, but a servant of the living God filled with the Holy Spirit. And so he saw, with the insight of a prophet, the deadly atomic threat, the end of history toward which we are doubtless headed.

The First Splitting of the Atom

In December 1938, scientists at a Berlin research institute succeeded in performing an experiment which caused great astonishment in the scientific world. For the first time there occurred a splitting of an atom and a simultaneous transformation of elements. If Hitler had obtained atomic power at that time, the Second World War would have turned out differently. He would

The atomic explosion forced the unconquerable Japan to surrender.

not have hesitated to turn Europe into rubble and ashes. But God was once again merciful to the earth and postponed this awful world-wide judgment. Why did God prevent the Germans from building an atomic bomb which shortly thereafter was developed by the Americans? Because His patience is great, and He does not desire *"that any should perish, but that all should come to repentance."*

What is an Atom?

Many people ask this question, and its answer is important in order to better understand that which follows. All earthly matter, the stars, the sun and the moon consist of atoms of approximately 100 elements. For example, we call the smallest possible piece of iron an iron atom. Such an atom is unimaginably small. If one could arrange a hundred million (100,000,000) of such atoms on a string like pearls, we would have a pearl necklace whose length was only one centimeter! (½ inch!) Tiny atomic nuclei of such small dimensions were exploded in 1938. And today further experimentation is being carried out on these atomic nuclei. The "atomic" theme is becoming of more

Hiroshima. destroyed by Americans in the first atomic bomb blast in 1945.

immediate interest because the oil reserves are decreasing.

Atomic Fission is Not an Invention

The splitting of atoms frees a tremendous amount of energy. A few notes on the subject:

"One element can readily be transformed into another. This is called transmutation of elements. Gold can quite easily be made from mercury. But the amount of gold produced would not be worth the technical expenditure. On the other hand, completely new elements, which were previously unknown on earth, are produced in kilogram amounts (1 kg. = 2.2 lb.). And one of these was dropped on Japan as an atomic bomb, at Hiroshima, near the end of the war in 1945. This element, which originated at that time, is called plutonium. It is possible to split or fuse atoms, and in the process some mass is lost. In place of this mass, energy is released, the famous "atomic energy."

In order that we might know what is happening during atomic fission, one further comparison is given: When one kilogram of coal is burned, nine kWh of energy are produced. When one kilogram of hydrogen is converted into helium through atomic fusion, 180 million kWh of energy are produced —

twenty million times as much energy as in the coal example.

Atomic fission is not an invention: God has incorporated this energy within His creation!

Can Underground Atomic Tests Cause Earthquakes?

In spite of SALT I and II (and perhaps soon SALT III), America and the Soviet Union are feverishly continuing underground atomic tests. One of the most recent Russian underground tests occurred in southeastern Russia, near the Iranian border. On the day after this test there was a terrible earthquake in Iran which caused 25,000 deaths. This is no coincidence, because scientists have determined that this earthquake was caused by nothing other than this Soviet atomic test.

How and When Will It All End?

Not only do the two superpowers of East and West have the atomic bomb. No, France did not want to be left out. China has similarly become an atomic power. Also, poor India and Pakistan, Brazil, and now Israel, have the atomic bomb.

As was said, the first atomic bomb was dropped on Hiroshima on August 6, 1945. It

Two of the countless persons who lived only a short time after the nuclear catastrophe over Hiroshima and Nagasaki.

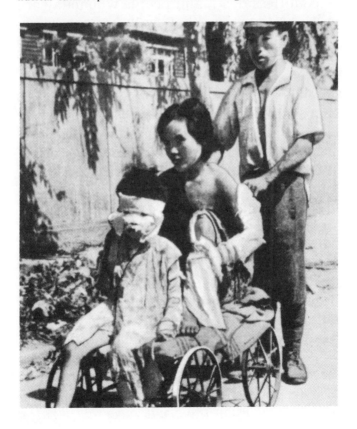

was only a comparatively small bomb containing barely one kilogram of uranium. But the results of this explosion were horrible — countless dead, and people who today are still disfigured. What will happen when thousands of such bombs of larger size are dropped in the East, West, South and North? In the last book of the Bible, John clearly describes the scene, for in Revelation 9 and 16 we read: *"By these three was the third part of men killed, by the fire, and by the smoke, and by the brimstone. And the fourth angel poured out his vial upon the sun; and power was given unto him to scorch men with fire. And men were scorched with great heat, and blasphemed the name of God, which hath power over these plagues: and they repented not to give him glory."* We can expect this nuclear confrontation in this generation because it will coincide with the judgment of all nations in Israel. Today all eyes are fixed upon Israel, because on account of Israel a worldwide nuclear catastrophe will be loosened. Where? At Armageddon. The Bible tells us about it: *"And the sixth angel poured out his vial upon the great river Euphrates;*

and the water thereof was dried up, that the way of the kings of the East (China, Japan and India) *might be prepared. And I saw three unclean spirits like frogs come out of the mouth of the dragon* (Satan) *and out of the mouth of the beast* (the Antichrist) *and out of the mouth of the false prophet* (Antispirit). *For they are spirits of devils, working miracles, which go forth unto the kings of the earth and of the whole world, to gather them to the battle of the great day of God Almighty. And he gathered them together into a place called in the Hebrew tongue Armageddon."* This is all coming.

Will Antisemistism Be Punished?

Advances in nuclear technology run parallel with increasing worldwide anti-Semitism, so they have a very close connection. He who has ears, let him hear! As all the nations march against Jerusalem, a nuclear catastrophe will be loosened. The living bodies of people will decay because of radiation sickness. And exactly those people will be punished who, because of their anti-Semitism, have marched against Jerusalem: *"And this shall be the plague wherewith the Lord will smite all the people that have fought*

The Euphrates River, the extreme northern border which protects Israel from the enemy nations of the world. At the final battle of the nations, the Euphrates will dry up, according to Revelation 16:12.

against Jerusalem; their flesh shall consume away while they stand upon their feet, and their eyes shall consume away in their holes, and their tongue shall consume away in their mouth" (Zechariah 14:12). Zechariah prophesied this in the sixth century B.C. Will it be fulfilled? Certainly!

Worldwide Fear of the Future

Today in world politics people speak of a balance of power (terror). And of what does this balance consist? It consists of the fact that the East and West each have approximately 100,000 nuclear bombs ready to guarantee "peace." But this is the big lie. Today we live on this earth as upon a volcano which, at any moment, could spew out its glowing mass of lava. Jesus was referring to our day when He said: *"Men's hearts failing them for fear, and for looking after those things which are coming on the earth: for the powers of heaven shall be shaken."* Everything is in a state of flux. The best-intentioned protest marches cannot force the wheel of time to run backward. Man of today is ruled more and more by a fear of the future. That is why there are so many depressed people today, and it is also why psychotherapists and psychiatrists are swamped with patients. They have so much work they cannot keep up with it. In West Germany alone there are, right now, six million mentally-ill persons. And the psychiatrists and psychotherapists have come to the point where they "simply cannot handle it." That is our time. We anxiously ask: "What is going to happen?"

Some are afraid they will have an auto accident, others fear a heart attack, while still others fear cancer or atomic war. These are nothing but realities which can create fear in thinking people. Bismark, the

German Chancellor, is supposed to have one time said: "We Germans fear God, and nothing else in the world." I doubt very much that this is true. But today we can say: Most of humanity does not fear God, but we certainly fear everything else.

The kings of the east are re-arming: battle-ready Japanese brigades.

The Most Basic Cause of All Fear

There are truly many things we are justified in fearing, but the cause of all fear is your destroyed relationship with the living God. Or to say it in "old-fashioned" words, which modern Bible translators have replaced with more acceptable words: The most basic cause of all fear is *sin*. Why? The Bible tells us that Adam, the first man, lived in complete peace with God. To him fear was a foreign word. But when he sinned, fear crept into his life, too, and we hear him say to God: *"I heard thy voice in the garden, and I was afraid."* This is your problem, because fear destroyed your relationship with God! This is why you fear the future, either consciously or unconsciously.

Is Sin Really So Bad?

Today's threat of nuclear war is a gigantic, ghost-like consequence of that which happened about 6,000 years ago in Paradise. That is when Satan succeeded in causing a split between God and man.

Before the fall from grace, a wonderful harmony existed between God and His

Volcanic eruption: Today we are living on a worldwide volcano which could suddenly spew out its glowing masses of lava.

creatures. Just listen to what the Creator Himself thought about His creation: *"And God saw everything that he had made, and, behold, it was* **very good.***"* Before Satan, in the form of the serpent, tempted man, and man sinned for the first time, man was one with God: one in nature, i.e., sinless, and one in his existence, i.e., eternal. But it was exactly this state of being one with God that was a thorn in Satan's eye. And by means of his lying question: *"Yea, hath God said . . .?"* he put doubt about God's word into man's heart and led him to sin. Through this split which Satan caused, a tremendous amount of energy was set free, namely, the destructive power of sin. Why this split? Because God's holiness and sin are at complete antipathy with one another.

Have you ever thought about what a demoralizing and destructive power sin is? The Bible speaks of the wages of sin: *"For the wages of sin is death."* Perhaps you say: Yes, if Adam sinned, it will not mean at all that I am guilty! But the Bible has an answer for this, too. It says: *"Wherefore, as by one man sin entered into the world; and so death passed upon all men, for that all have sinned."* Why is the history of the human race full of blood and tears? Because all have sinned!

Agents of a Higher Power

In the section entitled "Atomic Fission is Not an Invention" we have seen that a new element comes into being when an atom is split. That is what happened when man split off from God. Before the fall from grace, there was unity between God and man. Afterward there arose a new connection: man, Satan and sin. And so man became an agent of a higher power, Satan's power. Man, as a sinless element, was transformed into an element of sin by this splitting. Your powerlessness vis-a-vis sin and Satan resides in this transformation, and therefore you must lament: *"For the good that I would I do not: but the evil which I would not, I do. O wretched man that I am! who shall deliver me from the body of this death?"* But in saying this, you concede that you have been blended with destructive elements which drag you downward — and these are sin, death and the devil. Truly: there is nothing new under the sun, because there in the garden of Eden there

"And God saw everything that he had made, and, behold, it was very good" (Genesis 1:31).

occurred the first "splitting of the atom" in a spiritual area.

God's Great, "But"

As we have seen, sin is the element which separates God and man. Man is eternally separated from the holy God by indwelling sin. But the loving God did not simply leave humanity in Satan's hand, for we read in the Bible: *"But God, who is rich in mercy, for his great love wherewith he loved us, even when we were dead in sins, hath quickened us together in Christ."* This "us" refers to all who believe in Jesus, *"For God so loved the world, that he gave his only begotten Son, that whosoever believeth in him should not perish, but have everlasting life."*

God's Son, Jesus Christ, completed the saving "atomic fission" by His bloody death on the cross of Calvary where He bore the sin of the world and Himself was made sin. His sacrificial death on the cross freed powerful renewing energy so that the apostle Paul could triumphantly write to the Christians in Rome: *"But where sin abounded, grace did much more abound."*

Jesus' Blood — the Saving Element

When Jesus hung on the cross and bore the sin of the world, the entire universe was involved. But this spiritual atomic fission happened for your and my salvation. What happened as Jesus suffered torture and bitter death on the cross? Matthew reports that a darkness came over the entire land and that *"The earth did quake, and the rocks rent."* Was this not like an atomic explosion? What powerful forces were set free through Jesus' death, but not only in nature, but also for your and my redemption!

What power will enable you, who has become an element of sin, death and the devil, to again split off from it and to be connected to God? The precious blood of Jesus. You may now ask: Why does Jesus' blood have such great power? God Himself answers this question in the Old Testament: *"For the life of the flesh is in the blood: and I have given it to you upon the altar to make an atonement for your souls: for it is the blood that maketh an atonement for the soul."* Therefore Jesus Christ poured out His eternal life in His blood and gave it as an atonement upon God's altar.

Thus the power of Jesus' blood has the strength to transform a child of Satan into a child of God. Therefore you may come confidently to Jesus, call to Him and tell Him your sins!

Or do you think you are without sin? For example, adultery is a serious sin to God. You say: I have never committed adultery! But I tell you: How often have you committed adultery with your eyes and in your fantasy? Jesus said: *"Whosoever looketh on a woman to lust after her hath committed adultery with her already in his heart."* Have you always been honest and friendly toward everyone? Or have you ever hated anyone? In God's view, thoughts of hate are not without sin, because He says in His word: *"Whosoever hateth his brother is a murderer."* Except for Jesus, there never was, nor will there ever be, anyone without sin.

Stop playing hide-and-seek! God knows you better than you know yourself! He knows that you need Jesus who bore your sins. Do you now want to accept Jesus as your Saviour, who poured out His blood for you? He is waiting longingly for you to act. Call to Him and say: "Lord Jesus, I now accept you as my Saviour. Forgive my sins! I thank You that Your blood cleanses me from all sin." Now, believe firmly that He has actually forgiven you and has become your very personal Saviour! The Bible says: *"But as many as received him, to them gave he power to become the sons of God, even to them that believe on his name,"* and *"If we confess our sins, he is faithful and just to forgive us our sins, and to cleanse us from all unrighteousness,"* and *"And the blood of Jesus Christ his Son cleanseth us from all sin."*

Chapter IV

Escape for Thy Life!

Today we live in a catastrophic time! Depravation is increasing steadily. Thousands upon thousands of marriages break up yearly, and before long the one-time marriage partners are "married" to someone else. Homosexuality is being legalized; rape, murder and terror are the order of the day.

Thousands of years ago there was a similar situation. This was just before Sodom and Gomorrah were destroyed by fire. Today the Dead Sea covers these two cities. At that time a believer by the name of Lot lived in Sodom, along with his family. He was Abraham's nephew. Moral turpitude had reached its nadir — homosexuality was the usual thing. The eternal God watched these goings on for a certain time, because He has great patience, and He *"is not willing that any should perish, but that all should come to repentance."* But when His patience had been exhausted, and the time for the end of these cities had come, God told His faithful Abraham His plan. Abraham, knowing his nephew, Lot, was in mortal danger, prayed hard for him. At Abraham's fervent request, the Lord sent His two angels of judgment to Lot to warn him of the approaching judgment. They commanded him to lead all of his relatives out of the city and to take them to safety. Lot then went immediately to his sons-in-law and told them: *"Up, get you out of this place; for the Lord will destroy this city."* But they laughed at him and said he had told them a bad joke.

But It Was No Joke . . .

Because early the next morning, as the Bible tells us, the angels said: *"Arise, take thy wife, and thy two daughters, which are here; lest thou be consumed in the iniquity of the city. And while he lingered, the man laid hold upon his hand, and upon the hand of his wife, and upon the hand of his two daughters; the Lord being merciful unto him: and they brought him forth, and set him without the city. And it came to pass, when they had brought them forth abroad, that he said: Escape for thy life; look not behind thee, neither stay thou in all the plain; escape to the mountain, lest thou be*

The spirit of Sodom is spreading today: mass demonstration of homosexuals in Amsterdam.

consumed." But Lot thought he knew of a better place to go, and he asked to be permitted to go to the small town of Zoar. He was given permission to do so, and he was commanded: *"Haste thee, escape thither; for I cannot do any thing till thou be come thither."* Shortly after sunrise Lot reached Zoar, and as soon as he was safe, *"The Lord rained upon Sodom and upon Gomorrah brimstone and fire from the Land out of heaven; And he overthrew those cities, and all the plain, and all the inhabitants of the cities, and that which grew upon the ground."* Lot heeded the warning and was saved, but his sons-in-law, who laughed about the announcement of judgment, were killed (cf. Genesis 19).

God Speaks Today, Too

Lot was commanded: *"Escape for thy life,"* or, as another Bible translation says: *"Flee for your life."* God speaks to people. He wants to talk to you, too through these lines. Although the command, *"Flee for your life"* came to Lot by way of God's chosen messenger, it was, nevertheless, He who spoke through His angel. It is true that God's angels do not proclaim the Gospel, because man is appointed to do that.

Today God also speaks through His messengers who deliver such brief and urgent messages as "Escape for thy life!" "Flee for your life!" Or: "Save yourself, it is a matter of life and death!"

God is love. He loved Lot, and for that reason He saved him from Sodom as it was about to perish. God loves you, too. Just like Lot, we today live in "Sodom."

Sodom perished for the sin of destructive morality: homosexuality, perverseness, stealing, murder, greed and covetousness. In our days we are actually living in "Sodom," because just like then, homosexuality is in the process of being legalized. Governmental officials are more and more surrendering their authority, and they are becoming weaker and weaker in respect to the growing crime rate.

"Flee for your life!" There is absolutely no doubt that God's message of love, "Flee for your life!" was not announced in an indifferent tone of voice, but in a serious tone. Certainly, Lot was given preference by the fact that two of God's angels came to him

"But his wife looked back from behind him, and she became a pillar of salt" (Genesis 19:26).

personally to warn him of the impending judgment. But I say to you: You, too, are being given preference, because God is speaking to your heart. "For the sake of your eternal life, flee to Jesus!"

I do not know how angels speak, for I have

never heard an angel. But I am sure their whole heart was in it as they urged Lot: *"Flee for your life!"* I cannot say whether they whispered it into his ear, or if they called it out loudly. At any rate, this short message was so powerful that it saved Lot and his family. It had an immediate effect on the man who heard it, because he obeyed this command. May God give you grace to obey this command: *"Flee for your life!,"* because God does not desire the death of sinners; He wants them to be converted and live eternally.

Where Are We Today?

In Lot's time, Abraham, the first Israelite, the father of the Israeli people, appeared on the horizon. This resulted in the judgment of Sodom and Gomorrah. Today we are seeing the emergence of an entire nation, Israel, the offspring of Abraham. But this means the destruction of the nations, the judgment of the people. For this reason this *"Flee for your life!"* has special validity for the time in which we live.

Lot, who lived in a city ripe for judgment,

Abraham said to Lot: *"If thou depart to the right hand, then I will go to the left. And Lot lifted up his eyes, and beheld all the plain of Jordan"* (Genesis 13:9-10).

was not at all aware of the seriousness of the situation. He had no idea that there was no salvation for him and his family in Sodom.

I do not know where you are today, but I can say to you with certainty: If you are not in Christ, you are lost, and there is no salvation for you in eternity.

Decide!

How did Lot happen to come to Sodom? Was he a non-believer? Was he a heathen? No, that cannot be said of him, for the Bible calls him the "rightious Lot." But Lot was half-hearted. He knew God through his uncle, Abraham; but he had never made a personal decision for the Lord.

When Abraham lived in Haran, the Lord commanded him: *"Get thee out of thy country, and from thy kindred, and from thy father's house, unto a land that I will shew thee."*

Abraham followed God's call. We read in the Bible: *"So Abram departed, as the Lord had spoken unto him;* **and Lot went with him.**" This means that Lot did not personally let God's call have an effect on him. He left the fateful decision of whether he should emigrate to his uncle Abraham. When

Abraham left his realtives, Lot simply went along without personally reaching a decision. That was a serious sin of omission which Lot

May 14, 1948: David Ben Gurion proclaims the establishment of the state of Israel.

did not make up for later, either. He never said: "Lord, here am I." From a New Testament point of view, we would call Lot a

"Christian without Christ."

The Christian world is full of such fellow-travelers. There are many people who have been going to church for a long time who are probably baptized or confirmed, but who have never taken the most important step: You have not yet made a personal decision for Christ! But that is exactly what it all depends on! That is the only way you can become a child of God! That is what it says in John 1:12. As a person who has never decided for Christ, you are committing the same sin of omission as did Lot. But there is no salvation for you if you continue to be a fellow-traveler. This sin of omission, not to have made a personal decision for the Lord is what, in the final analysis, brought Lot to this city of Sodom which was ripe for judgment, and thereby, into extreme mortal danger. Nor can **you** put off any longer making this long-overdue decision for or against the Lord. Flee to Jesus for the sake of your eternal life!

Omission Leads to a
Dangerous Compromise

If you persist in this sin of omission, if you think things will be fine without making a personal decision for Christ, then I must tell you: You are in a dangerous situation, because the sin of omission always leads to the sin of compromise. Naturally Lot was a believer, but not with all his heart. With people who, in respect to God's Word, have not yet made their life's decision for the invisible Lord, it is always the same. In their later life, they are never able to make decisions based on God's Word, but they will always look for support in their calculations to what they can see. This is also the way Lot was.

When God called Abraham to move to a strange country, he was already 75 years old, and his wife was 65. But the Lord added a "P.S." to Abraham: *"I will make of thee a great nation."* Now at that time Abraham had no children. He doubtless believed in God's ability to give him and his wife children in their old age, but in case his faith was not great enough, he thought: *"I will take my dear* nephew Lot on this trip. *"And Lot went with him."* But when they reached the Promised Land, settled down and their herds had greatly increased in size, we read: *"And the land was not able to bear them, that they might*

"Only divine shoulders could bear this burden."

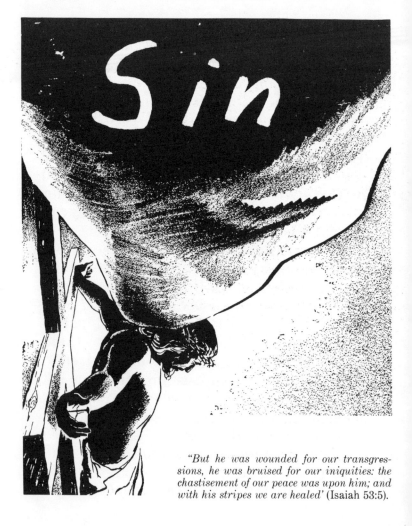

"But he was wounded for our transgressions, he was bruised for our iniquities: the chastisement of our peace was upon him; and with his stripes we are healed" (Isaiah 53:5).

dwell together." The day came when they had to separate. This is when the conflict in the Middle East had its very beginning. Abraham allowed his nephew to choose freely where he wanted to move, and we read in the Bible how he decided: *"And Lot lifted up his eyes, and beheld all the plain of Jordan, that is was well watered everywhere, before the Lord destroyed Sodom and Gomorrah, even as the garden of the Lord, like the land of Egypt, as thou comest unto Zoar. Then Lot chose him all the plain of Jordan; and Lot journeyed east: and they separated themselves the one from the other."* Lot therefore made his decision on the basis of what he saw. From a "business" point of view Lot's choice was completely in order. He could have decided in no other way. Yes, he lifted up his eyes, but he did not see the invisible Lord, but he saw that which was visible. But Abraham looked up and prayed to the Lord, as he later testified to the king of Sodom: *"I have lift up mine hand unto the Lord, the most high God, the possessor of heaven and earth."*

Lot now settled down with his family in Sodom. But even here this believer was a friend of compromise, because when his two daughters considered becoming engaged to two men of Sodom, he had no authority to say no. Thus the spirit of Sodom entered his family, and what was the consequence?

No Strength of Conviction

As the angels of God stood before Lot and implored him: *"Flee for your life!"* he hurried, as was mentioned, to his sons-in-law, but his earnest attempt to save these two men of Sodom was not successful. As we already saw, they laughed at him as he predicted the imminent destruction of Sodom and begged them to flee from the city. Lot's readiness to compromise caused his testimony to have no strength of conviction. If you are a Christian with an ambivalent heart, if you limp along on both sides of the issue like Lot, then your witness for Jesus will have a ridiculous effect. Or if you make your decisions on the basis of what you see, and do not build on the Word of the invisible God, then your attempts to bring others to Jesus will fail. Unbelievers seldom make fun of people who tell them about Jesus, but they begin to make fun when they notice that you do not live as you would have them

You, too, are living in the midst of "Sodom," and judgment will break in upon you suddenly (Dresden, Germany, 1945).

believe you live by means of your testimony.

The End of Unbelief

Anyone who lives like Lot in the sin of half-heartedness and indecision has no security of salvation for eternity. This is why this message now thunders toward you: *"Flee for your life!"*

I remember one revival in Europe. Because of the message, many came to the Lord. One man in the audience was a government official. When he heard the call, "Please come forward if you want to accept Jesus," he started to stand up, but a voice within him said: "No, no!" and he sat down again. That was on a Saturday — and on Monday he was dead. This man did not want to hear the call. Lot hesitated, too. When one of the angels told him to hurry, he told him: *"No, Lord!"* I would like to tell you again: There is no safety, no salvation, in unbelief. Lot's inner orientation was unbelief. In the final analysis he believed more in what he saw than in Him, Whom he did not see. With Paul it was just the opposite. He testified of the believing Corinthians and of himself: *"While we look not at the things which are seen, but at the things which are not seen."* Although Lot's wife was already safely outside of Sodom, she looked back — and became a pillar of salt. She was unable to free herself from that which is visible. This looking at that which is earthly later caused fearful ruin and destruction in Israel after the people had happily escaped from slavery in Egypt. And exactly the same thing will happen to today's manipulated consumer TV society which is geared to what it seeks in the visible world. But in this way man will be blunted toward the Lord and sink slowly into ever-deepening unbelief until death overtakes him.

Faith's Breakthrough

In Sodom, Lot found himself in semi-darkness. That is why he was shocked when the message of judgment suddenly reached him. This happened at a point in time when he neither saw nor suspected disaster, because before the angels came to him the sky was blue and the sun shone beautifully. But now he heard: *"Flee for your life!"* He had a choice between two things: Either to believe the message or to doubt it. But thank God Lot believed, and was saved.

Friend, we do not yet see, either. Everything is just like before. After the storm the clouds blow away, and the sun breaks through again. Everything seems in good order: You have your steady income; you actually lack nothing. You still believe what you see. But I tell you today, as a messenger of Christ: *"Flee for your life,"* because everything you see, and from which you live, will quickly and suddenly collapse.

Self-righteousness is
No Life Preserver

Lot would have had reason to boast about his morals because he disassociated himself from the sin of homosexuality. Peter later mentioned in one of his letters that Lot suffered inwardly. In spirit he was no Sodomite, but in spite of this he had a seat on the Sodom city council, so he was enmeshed in this filth against his will. This is the way it is with you. You can renounce and give up many things, for example, you can stop smoking because of health reasons. You may be an upright citizen who drinks a glass of wine only now and then. You may be

How much time do you still have? Flee to Jesus for the sake of your life!

respected in your circle of friends. You may
even have an official position in your town
like Lot. Nevertheless, you are in the devil's
claws! Why? Pay particular attention to what
was said to Lot: *"Escape for thy life; look not
behind thee, neither stay thou in all the plain,
escape to the mountain, lest thou be consumed."*

Escape to the Mountain

When I read this call of the angel to Lot:
*"Escape to the mountain, lest thou be
consumed,"* I hear the sounds of the Gospel.
The angels said to him, as it were: You cannot
stay in this city of corruption, you must flee to
this mountain. And I tell you now; You cannot
remain as you are, vegetating and waiting
until it is eternally too late for you. No —
escape to the mountain, to the hill of Calvary,
where God, in Jesus Christ, reconciled the
world to Himself! Flee for the sake of your
eternal life to where the Lord Jesus has borne
away your sins and mine!

Parting is Painful, But . . .

Let us regard this matter from another
perspective: if Lot wanted to be saved, then
he had to hurry, break off his good relations

and leave his friends at a moment's notice.
Anyone who flees to Jesus will lose many
friendships. Several years ago, I was pro-
claiming a message of salvation through
Jesus in a church. A young communist came
to the Lord. When he wanted to come to the
meeting next evening, his friends accom-
panied him to the church door, talking
earnestly to him, doing all they could to
persuade him not to go. But the young man
had courage: He chose Jesus, he became a
happy child of God — and lost all his former
friends. But in their place he won a hearty
fellowship with the many brothers and
sisters of the church, and new, permanent
friendships were formed.

Lot had to make a choice, too, between
eternal life and his many friendships. He
must certainly have been a good businessman
and had a beautiful house with all the
trimmings. Now he was faced with making a
decision which was of vital importance —
either to give up everything or to lose
everything, including his life. Question: Are
you ready to give up everything in order to
save yourself? Tear yourself loose from your

comfort and your lack of resolve: Flee to the mountain for the sake of your eternal life! Hurry to Calvary! You are living in the midst of "Sodom," and judgment will suddenly break in upon you. We are living in a time which is ripe for judgment, and I call to you as seriously as I can: "Flee for the sake of your eternal life, escape to the mountain!" Let us assume Lot remained in Sodom on account of his house, his pleasant friendships and his savings account. What would have happened? On the very same day he would have lost everything, including his own life. Listen to the voice of Jesus: *"For what is a man profited, if he shall gain the whole world, and lose his own soul?"* If you remain in your sins, then if you should die, or the Lord should suddenly appear, you can take absolutely nothing with you that you are still hanging onto so tightly. The Bible says: *"For we brought nothing into this world, and it is certain we can carry nothing out."* That is the shortest biography of your whole life.

Eternal Pangs of Conscience

If Lot had remained in Sodom, he would have perished with all the Sodomites. let us consider practically what that would have meant: Lot would have been lost, although he could have been saved by the warning. While the flames would have been engulfing him, the thought would have come to him: "I was ordered to flee, but I did not do it. I was led out of the city. I was almost saved, but I turned back. I had the rare opportunity to be saved by God's messengers — but I did not seize it. Now it is too late! Such thoughts will torture those who are lost throughout eternity, those who could have permitted themselves to be saved. Flee for the sake of your eternal life! Hurry to Jesus in order that you may not destroy yourself and be lost for eternity! The Bible says: *"He that hath the Son hath life; and he that hath not the Son of God hath not life."*

Secure in Jesus for Eternity

When I think of all the millions of Chinese, Indians, South Americans, etc., who have not yet heard the Gospel! They can go to heaven only if they hear of Jesus and accept Him. You will not go to heaven without Jesus, either. But your damnation will be so much

more horrible, and your lostness so much
more fearful than that of those who never
heard of the Saviour, because you heard it all,
and although you were brought so near to
God by hearing His Word proclaimed, you
still remain far from Him. Oh, I beg God that
He will move your heart to flee to Jesus' arms
for the sake of your eternal bliss. I know that
you long for this security. You have no
certainty that you are a child of God, and this
uncertainty is gnawing at your heart. Its
source is the fact that you have not yet sought
refuge in Jesus. You have not yet said to Him:
"Lord Jesus, I come to You. I accept you as my
Saviour. Forgive my sins. I thank You that
You have shed Your blood for me."

Hesitate No Longer!

If God loved us so much that He saw no
other way to save you and me than to send His
only-begotten Son to death on the cross, then
sin must be extremely serious. Therefore:
Flee to Jesus for the sake of your eternal life!
But if you do not want to do this, then in your
life there remains an open question which no
one can answer, and for which neither the
Bible nor the angels, or even God Himself can

provide an answer. This question is: "How will you escape if you neglect such great salvation?"

Lot had a special privilege. Apart from the fact that he heard the message of salvation so clearly, he had a further advantage: His uncle Abraham prayed for him. I am convinced that among my readers there are those who have the same advantage. It may be that your wife, your husband, one of your children, a friend or someone else is praying for you, and you are not aware of it. You may say: "My mother or my father may have prayed for me, but they are dead now." But I tell you: Their prayers are not dead. God can still hear them.

"Flee for your life!" This short, urgent message reached Lot at a special time: On that day on which the city of Sodom was destroyed. That was Lot's second advantage, the very last possibility of saving his life by fleeing from Sodom. Among the readers of this message, there are probably people to whom God is offering, for the last time, an opportunity to flee to Jesus with their sins. In Lot's life there was one more dangerous

moment. He hesitated, and even said: *"Oh, not so, my Lord!"* Lot wavered back and forth like a reed in the wind. But this short, serious message had a very special power because it came directly from God to Lot by way of the angel. And Lot let himself be saved!

"Escape for thy life. Escape to the mountain, lest thou be consumed." I have implored God to give this message which you have read (perhaps it is the last warning for you) the special power of the Holy Spirit.

Lot had to go a certain distance before reaching Zoar. But you need not go very far, because the Lord is very near to you right now. He is standing at the door of your heart and is waiting for you to finally open it. The risen Jesus says to you: *"Behold, I stand at the door and knock: if any man hear my voice, and open the door, I will come in to him, and will sup with him, and he with me."* Should you not flee to Him now and be saved for eternity?

By The Same Author

There Shall Be Signs from 1948-1982

Wim Malgo   **$2.95**

"There shall be signs in the sun, and in the moon, and in the stars, and upon the earth distress among nations." These words spoken by our Lord Jesus Christ in Jerusalem, Israel are the basis of this book.

What are these signs? Could the alignment of the planets, predicted by scientists for 1982, be part of the fulfillment?

Be sure to order this truly fascinating end-time book today! Order extra copies for friends and relatives!

3 books: $7.00   10 books: $15.00   15 books: $20

Russia's Last Invasion

Wim Malgo   **$2.95**

When will it happen? *"In the latter years thou shalt come into the land that is brought back from the sword, and is gathered out of many people, against the mountains of Israel"* (Ezekiel 38:8). From these immovable statements, the author shows in unmistakably clear terms, how the latest world political movements are developing exactly according to the prophetic statements of the Bible.

3 books: $7.00   10 books: $15.00

Called to Pray

Wim Malgo   **$2.95**

An enlightening and reliable guide to a victorious prayer-life. Read in this book how Prophets, Apostles, Priests and Kings used PRAYER to overcome the enemy. Tells how your life in Christ can become a powerful testimony. PRAYER is one of the most important subjects in your Bible. 17 inspiring chapters to fill your heart! A real treasure in every Christian home.

2 books: $5.00   3 books: $7.00   10 books: $15.00

Biblical Counseling

Wim Malgo $3.95

Biblical Counseling is the title of Dr. Malgo's book which contains over 260 questions and answers selected from his 30 years of Counseling Ministry. This book is highly recommended for Ministers, Counselors, and serious Christians. It makes an ideal gift for any occasion. Order extra copies today!

2 books for $6.00   **4 books for $10.00**

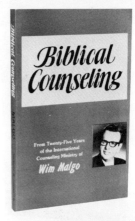

Israel Shall Do Valiantly

Wim Malgo $2.95

A book which makes Prophecy come alive! Over 3400 years ago it was said: "Israel Shall Do Valiantly" today this Prophecy has become a visible reality in the Middle East. Wim Malgo expounds Biblically the Holy Land and it's people from the old past to the present and into the future. Isreael, the uncomparable and most astonishing nation of this century. Some of the chapters in this book include . . . Israel's origin, calling, tragedy and future . . . Russia's miscalculation and Israel . . . The connection between space travel, nuclear threat and Israel . . . Is the Antichrist already among us? . . . The last two witnesses before worldwide catastrophe . . . and other vital subjects.

2 books: $5.00   **3 books: $7.00**   **10 books: $15.00**

Shadows of Armageddon

Wim Malgo $3.95

What began in 1948 in the Middle East as a seemingly insignificant local matter has taken on worldwide proportions today. The author shows in unmistakably clear terms that even political conflicts such as Vietnam and Cyprus are definitely signs of the preparation for the battle of Armageddon.

2 books: $6.00   **4 books: $10.00**

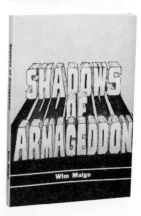

Israel's God Does Not Lie

Wim Malgo $3.95

This book is a must for every serious Christian, who is waiting for the Second Coming of Christ. The author penetrates deeply into the Spiritual background of the latest events in the Middle East, including the "Yom Kippur War." Illuminating these events in the light of Biblical Prophecy, many astonishing truths are clearly revealed as never before.

Some of the Chapters contained in this book:
- The Yom Kippur War
- Jerusalem's Border
- Will the Antichrist come from the tribe of Dan?
- The Destruction of the Nations
- The First and the Last King of Jerusalem
- ... and more.

2 books: $6.00   4 books: $10.00

1000 Years of Peace . . . A Utopia?

Wim Malgo $2.95

A refreshing outline on the much debated subject — the millennium. Without discussion and argument the author goes directly to the source — the Bible, to show the clear teaching of the coming 1000 years peace. The millennium is the answer to Jesus' prayer, "Thy Kingdom Come." The patriarchs, prophets, kings and priests looked forward to the thousand year reign of peace.

Some of the chapters in this book: Israel's position in the millennium ... Where will the church be during the millennium? ... What will happen after the millennium?

2 books: $5.00   3 books: $7.00   10 books: $15.00

The Last Days

Wim Malgo $2.95

Each day the Church is drawing closer to the day when the "fullness of the Gentiles be come in" which will climax into the RAPTURE of all born-again believers. This book gives a clear Biblical answer to why the battle in the invisible world is the reason for the near-chaos condition of the world today.

3 books: $7.00   10 books: $15.00

Prayer and Revival

Wim Malgo   **$3.95**

What can we do to cause a Revival? How does a Revival begin? Does God want to send a Revival? There are divine conditions we must first meet in order to have Revival. Analyzing these conditions for Revival through the Bible, this book will help serious Christians to find the pathway to Revival.

2 books: $6.00   **4 books: $10.00**

50 Questions Most Frequently Asked About the Second Coming

Wim Malgo   **$2.95**

Biblical answers revealed to topical questions . . .
- Will America become Communist?
- Who is the Antichrist?
- Will Israel join Ecumenical Movement?
- How will the Rapture take place?
- Must the Church go through the Great Tribulation?
- Why did Czechoslovakia not defend herself against Russia?
- Can we expect a nuclear war? . . . and 43 more vital questions answered — **essential for every one waiting for the Second Coming!**

2 books: $5.00   **3 books: $7.00**   **10 books: $15.00**

Jerusalem Focal Point of the World

Wim Malgo   **$2.95**

Jerusalem is not just another city — it is the city of God, the future capital of the world. This city is unequaled in the history of mankind and is today back in the spotlight of the world.

The Arabs claim Jerusalem, so does the Catholic Church and the United Nations . . . but God has a different plan!

Some of the chapters in this book:
- Jerusalem Focal Point of World Peace
- God's Oath Concerning Jerusalem
- Rome versus Jerusalem
- The Significance of the Number 666
- The heavenly Jerusalem

2 books: $5.00   **3 books: $7.00**   **10 books: $15.00**

THE RAPTURE

by Wim Malgo 95c

This booklet gives light on . . . How will it happen? . . . who will take part? . . . what must I do? . . . and many other important questions answered.

VALUABLE FOR BIBLE STUDY

SEVEN SIGNS OF A BORN AGAIN PERSON

by Wim Malgo 95c

A crystal clear outline how to recognize a truly born-again person. Answers vital questions every one should know.

SEVEN BIBLICAL SIGNS

ON THE BORDER OF TWO WORLDS

by Wim Malgo 95c

Tells how a Christian can keep the victory in his daily walk with Christ. Subjects included: In Enemy Territory . . . The Great WHY . . . Religious Deception . . . False Spirits . . . Demonic Bonds . . . Victory in Everyday Life . . . and more.

ORDER FORM

Fill in, Clip, and Mail This Whole Page to:

Midnight Call, P.O. Box 864, Columbia, SC 29202

How Many	Title		Total Price
_____	Russia's Last Invasion	$2.95	_____
_____	Shadows of Armageddon	$3.95	_____
_____	There Shall Be Signs From 1948 to 1982	$2.95	_____
_____	50 Questions About the Second Coming	$2.95	_____
_____	Prayer and Revival	$3.95	_____
_____	The Last Days	$2.95	_____
_____	Jerusalem — Focal Point of the World	$2.95	_____
_____	Israel's God Does Not Lie	$3.95	_____
_____	1000 Years Peace	$2.95	_____
_____	Israel Shall Do Valiantly	$2.95	_____
_____	Called To Pray	$2.95	_____
_____	The Rapture	$.95	_____
_____	Seven Signs of a Born-Again Person	$.95	_____
_____	Terrifying Goal of Ecumenical Movement	$.95	_____
_____	On The Border of Two Worlds	$.95	_____
_____	Group Dynamics, New Tool of the Antichrist	$.95	_____
_____	Signs and Wonders	$.95	_____
_____	Begin with Sadat	$1.95	_____
_____	Biblical Counseling	$3.95	_____
_____	How To Walk With God	$.95	_____
_____	Israel's Last Son	$.95	_____

Please send me a one-year subscription to:

☐ Midnight Call $4.00

☐ News From Israel $4.00

TOTAL ENCLOSED: _____

NAME: _____

ADDRESS: _____

CITY: _____ STATE: _____ ZIP: _____